Suicide

Look for these and other books in the Lucent Overview Series:

Suicide

by Adam Woog

LUCENT
BOOKS

LUCENT Overview Series

Library of Congress Cataloging-in-Publication Data

Woog, Adam.
    Suicide / by Adam Woog.
        p.   cm. — (Lucent overview series)
    Includes bibliographical references and index.
    Summary: Surveys the social phenomenon of suicide, its causes,
primary victims, and prevention.
    ISBN 1-56006-187-1 (alk. paper)
    1. Suicide—Juvenile literature.   2. Suicide—Prevention—
Juvenile literature. 3. Youth—Suicidal behavior—Juvenile literature.
[1. Suicide.]   I. Title.   II. Series.
HV6545.W75   1997
362.2'8—dc20   96-9855
                                                                            CIP
                                                                             AC

For my wife, Karen,
and in memory of my friend
Howard Broomfield.

Contents

INTRODUCTION   8

CHAPTER ONE   13
Why Do People Commit Suicide?

CHAPTER TWO   26
Teen Suicide

CHAPTER THREE   41
Is Suicide Ever an Acceptable Solution?

CHAPTER FOUR   52
After a Suicide

CHAPTER FIVE   68
Preventing Suicide

ORGANIZATIONS TO CONTACT   83
SUGGESTIONS FOR FURTHER READING   87
WORKS CONSULTED   89
INDEX   92
ABOUT THE AUTHOR   95
PICTURE CREDITS   96

Introduction

SUICIDE—CATASTROPHIC, HEARTBREAKING, and baffling—stands out as a large social issue. The tenth leading cause of death in the United States, suicide is indeed an urgent problem. About eighty people a day kill themselves in this country. That translates into about thirty thousand people each year, or one every eighteen minutes. The problem is especially severe among young people, who have the fastest growing suicide rate of any age group.

But each suicide is also a personal tragedy. A person who kills himself or herself is not the only victim of that act. Each suicide is like a stone thrown into a pond, setting in motion a ripple effect that changes forever the lives of dozens of people who will go on living. It has been estimated that a quarter million such people, sometimes called suicide survivors, are created every year.

Researchers, psychologists, and other professionals have tried for years to understand why some people are moved to take their own lives. It is hoped that with greater understanding, it will be possible both to reduce the near-epidemic proportions of suicide in our society and to cope more effectively and sensitively with the individual tragedy behind each suicide.

The patterns researchers find in statistics have yielded some important insights. Researchers can describe the type of person who is most likely to commit suicide, for example. They can also identify some of the common factors in the lives of those who attempt or successfully carry out suicide. By noticing these clues and acting on them, therapists and others can often prevent a needless death.

However, no one knows of a single reason or cause for suicide. There is no such thing as a "suicidal type." Suicide occurs in every possible group and division of humanity, in every culture in the world, in every period in history.

Factors in suicide

Worldwide, about one million people commit suicide every year. Suicide rates are measured per capita (per person) and annually (per year). Hungary has the highest per capita suicide rate of any country, according to the World Health Organization: 61.4 suicides per 100,000 people. The next highest rates are in Denmark, Austria, Finland, Switzerland, Sweden, Japan, and Germany. Some of the lowest rates are found in Italy, Spain, Ireland, and Mexico; Greece, with only 2.9 deaths per 100,000, has the lowest rate of any country.

The United States falls in the middle of this spectrum. Its rate of 12.7 per 100,000 people has held fairly steady since the late 1970s. Within the overall rate, researchers have identified some important distinctions.

Family members attend a funeral for two sisters who died in a suicide pact. Suicide's roots are complex and varied.

For reasons that are not clear, men commit about three-fourths of all completed suicides but women commit about three-fourths of all attempted (incomplete) suicides. Age, failing health, and loneliness are also factors. People sixty-five and over are more likely to kill themselves than those in other age groups. People who are widowed, divorced, separated, or living alone are at higher risk than married people. Older white single males have the highest suicide rate of all.

Work-related stress can add to the potential for suicide. People in high-stress professional positions are at great risk; medical doctors, for instance, commit suicide at a rate three times higher than the general population.

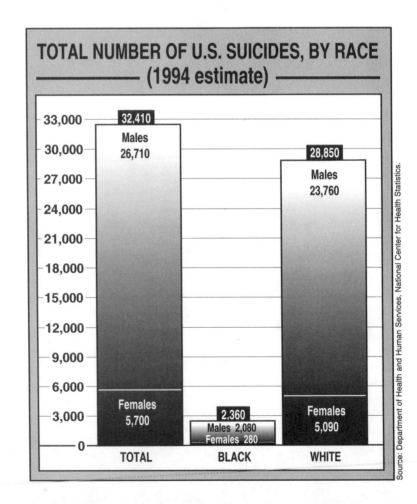

Source: Department of Health and Human Services, National Center for Health Statistics.

But work-related stress is also common among other economic and social groups; chronic unemployment, for instance, is a major factor in suicide statistics. Overall, the rich, the middle class, and the poor have roughly equal suicide rates.

In general, minorities in the United States have a suicide rate that is only about half that of the white population. Native Americans have the highest rate of all U.S. minority groups, perhaps as a result of the despair felt by many Native Americans trapped by poverty and alcoholism. The black population in this country, meanwhile, has a slightly lower rate than the average for minorities; it is especially low for elderly black people but dramatically higher for young black men in urban areas. Experts suggest this contrast may be due to the close ties most elderly African Americans have to church and community, whereas young African Americans frequently are estranged from these institutions.

Generally, suicides occur more frequently in the western states than elsewhere in the country. Nevada has the highest rate of any state—twice that of the nation as a whole. This may be because the gambling centers of Reno and Las Vegas tend to attract desperate people. Overall, cities, rural areas, and suburban areas have almost identical rates.

Researchers have identified many ways in which people kill themselves. The National Center for Health Statistics lists over forty general categories and many more variations. In America, more than half of all suicides are committed with guns. The next most common methods, in order, are hanging, drowning, poisoning, and jumping from high places. The United States is the only country in the world where guns are the primary means of suicide. Where firearm control laws are stiffer, other methods are more frequently used. For instance, in England asphyxiation using domestic cooking gas is number one; in other European countries, hanging is the most common method.

Even the seasons and the day of the week can be factors in suicide patterns. Most suicides occur in the spring. The rates tend to drop in winter; contrary to popular belief, they are not especially high during the holiday season. For some reason, more suicides occur on Monday than any other day of the week; the fewest occur on Saturday.

These are only some of the raw data that can be extracted from suicide statistics. But patterns of suicide are meaningless without an analysis of the reasons behind them. Any understanding of suicide as a social issue or as a personal tragedy must include not only *how* and *when* people commit suicide, but also *why*.

1

Why Do People Commit Suicide?

FOR THOUSANDS OF years, people have wondered about the reasons behind suicide. Many theories have been put forward. No one, however, has found a complete or satisfactory answer.

Each case of suicide is separate and individual, with its own complications, sorrows, and mysteries. There is no single explanation for what causes people to kill themselves. Writer George Howe Colt put it this way: "Trying to find the answer is like trying to pinpoint what causes us to fall in love or what causes war." And the distinguished psychoanalyst Karl Menninger, who spent much of his life studying suicide, once remarked, "It's a durn mystery, you know, in spite of all we've written about it."

Still, some progress has been made in understanding the roots and immediate causes of this disturbing social phenomenon. The ongoing research into the question falls into three rough categories: sociological, psychological, and biological studies. Sociological approaches try to explain suicide by examining how social groups can affect an individual's decision to kill himself or herself. Psychological views concentrate on the mental aspects, searching for an explanation within the workings of the mind. Biological methods, meanwhile, look at possible medical and physical causes of suicide.

Sociological theories

Sociology is the study of societies and cultures. Sociological studies of suicide, therefore, concentrate on how social structures and cultural rules can create an atmosphere that fosters self-destructive behavior—or, conversely, how they might prevent it.

The first major sociological study of suicide, still used as a basic model, was made by a Frenchman, Émile Durkheim, in 1897. Durkheim argued that two major factors affect the relationship between an individual and a social group. One is degree of regulation: the extent to which rules and codes of conduct control how people act within the group, leaving relatively little freedom of behavior. The other factor is the degree of the person's integration into the group; that is, how well he or she fits in. If these factors are balanced, the chance of suicide will be low. If there is imbalance, the chances will rise.

In the late nineteenth century, French sociologist Émile Durkheim pioneered the sociological study of suicide when he tried to identify factors that may contribute to suicidal behavior.

For example, an elderly man who has recently lost his wife, who sees his circle of friends shrinking as a result of aging and death, who has no children and few ties to his church or other groups might become increasingly lonely and isolated. This man might think of himself as not fitting into society anymore. He may see no reason to stay alive.

At the opposite extreme, too much integration in a group can foster suicide. Some people identify so closely with a group that they put the group's welfare above their own. For example, an ill woman who killed herself recently left behind a note stating her belief that she was a financial burden to others; she felt that her family would be better off with her gone.

Too many regulations and rules can also create a suicidal atmosphere. Highly structured societies can foster suicide if a person is so far out of step that there seems to be no other solution to complex and troublesome situations. This may help explain the relatively high suicide rates in

Thousands of fans mourned the death of singer Kurt Cobain, who ended his life at the age of twenty-seven. Cobain's suicide may have been triggered in part by the overwhelming popularity of his band Nirvana.

Japan and Austria, countries that place great emphasis on group order and social conformity. Imprisoned criminals who commit suicide rather than continue living as prisoners also fall into this category.

On the other hand, suicide can be the result of too few rules and regulations. A major upheaval in someone's life creates a chaotic world with no understandable rules about relationships, career, or health. A person who cannot handle these changes may become suicidal. Such changes are usually negative, such as the loss of a job or the death of someone close. But they can be positive and yet so unsettling that they disorient a person to the point of suicide.

Kurt Cobain was one victim of this kind of overwhelming stress. Bewildered and depressed by the massive popularity of his band Nirvana, the singer-guitarist shot himself in 1994, at the age of twenty-seven. In an obituary published in *Rolling Stone*, writer Anthony DeCurtis tried to pinpoint Cobain's conflicting emotions: "Seeing himself since his boyhood as an outcast, he was stunned—and confused, and frightened, and repulsed, and truth be told, not entirely disappointed (no one forms a band to remain anonymous)—to find himself a star."

Psychological theories

While sociology tries to analyze suicide by looking at outside influences, psychology views it from the inside. To psychologists, suicide is not caused by external events; it comes from within an individual. The groundwork for this field of research was laid by Sigmund Freud, the founder of psychoanalysis.

Freud suggested that inside every person is an instinct toward death. This unconscious emotion exists side by side with another instinct, one for survival. These deep-rooted feelings, Freud argued, are always in conflict. Usually the instinct for survival prevails; when it does not, a person commits suicide, or tries to.

Other psychologists and psychiatrists have expanded on Freud's ideas. One of his students, Alfred Adler, developed the theory of the inferiority complex. Adler argued that a feeling of inferiority or worthlessness can create a suicidal impulse. People who feel worthless often also feel they have no control over their own lives. A man who hanged himself left behind a note expressing the feeling that he could control nothing in his life, that he was at the mercy of everyone and everything. For him, suicide was the only way to control something; at least he could control his death.

Another of Freud's students, Karl Menninger, separated suicide into three categories. "Chronic" suicide involves long-term self-destructive behavior or mental illness. Seriously psychotic people as well as those who engage in such self-destructive behavior as alcoholism are considered to be chronic suicides. An "organic" suicide is one in which the decision to end life is a response to grave physical illness or pain. An AIDS patient who chooses suicide instead of a

long, painful exit falls into this category. A "focal" suicide, meanwhile, is a suicide (or suicide attempt) that is primarily a self-centered cry for help or attention from others. A person who repeatedly makes unsuccessful suicide attempts exemplifies the concept of focal suicide.

Biological theories

The third basic avenue for approaching the study of suicide, besides sociology and psychology, is neurobiology, or the study of biology with a focus on biological processes in the brain. An increasing amount of evidence indicates that physical or chemical disorders in the brain may be at the heart of at least some suicidal tendencies.

Specifically, research has focused on the role of a brain chemical called serotonin. Serotonin is a neurotransmitter, one of the chemical "messengers" that help the brain communicate signals to nerve cells and create thoughts and feelings. Studies of severely depressed people, and autopsies of the remains of people who have committed suicide, have shown abnormally low levels of serotonin.

Research indicates that in the absence of an adequate amount of serotonin, the brain's communication system breaks down. As a result, certain forms of depression and/or increased aggressiveness may occur. However, scientists do not yet understand exactly the link between low neurotransmitter levels and tendencies toward depression and aggression. There is no clear evidence demonstrating whether low serotonin levels are the cause of depression and aggressiveness, or simply a symptom of something deeper.

Low serotonin levels can often be controlled with the use of drug therapy. Antidepressant drugs have been used since the 1950s, and a number of new agents are now available. Most doctors and therapists consider these

Sigmund Freud revolutionized the field of psychology when he developed his theory of psychoanalysis. His work includes theories about the causes of suicide. Freud suggested that suicide is connected to an instinct toward death that, he believed, is inside every person.

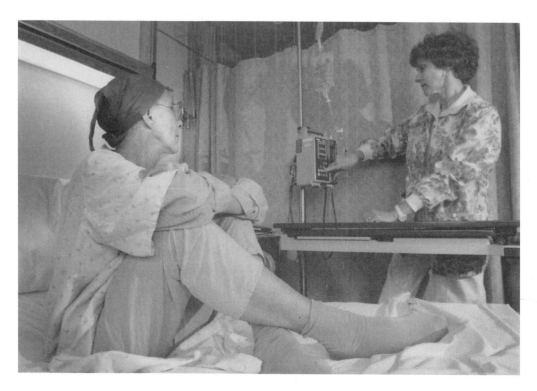

A sixty-three-year-old cancer patient receives treatment for her illness. Psychiatrist Karl Menninger classified suicides into categories; an "organic" suicide involves choosing to kill oneself rather than suffer a long, debilitating illness, such as cancer.

drugs to be an essential part of long-term therapy for suicidal people. Their use is controversial, however, in part because they may be accompanied by severe side effects.

Depression

Within the three broad research methods used to study suicide, several specific factors are closely linked. Such events or emotions affect a person's life severely enough to bring about a suicidal frame of mind. These so-called suicide triggers, taken alone, do not explain why people kill themselves. However, they can help researchers understand some of the motivating forces.

The most frequently identified suicide trigger is severe depression. Severe depression (sometimes called clinical, major, or unipolar depression) is the most common mental illness that leads to suicide.

Severe depression should not be confused with those periods of gloom that nearly everyone experiences at various points in life. Such "blue" periods pass quickly for most people, but not for those with severe depression. A person who is severely depressed has an illness that leads to an inability to escape gloomy thoughts and a constant feeling of hopelessness, dejection, and unworthiness.

Depression is closely linked to suicide, but this condition alone does not explain suicide. Studies indicate that for every person who commits suicide there are a thousand other depressed people. Although not everyone who commits suicide shows evidence of depression beforehand, the connection appears to be strong. Research suggests that over half of all suicides had a history of severe depression. The National Institute of Mental Health (NIMH) estimates that severely depressed people have a suicide rate twenty-five times higher than the general population. And it has been estimated that one in four Americans suffers from clinical depression at some point in his or her life.

In his study of suicide, *The Savage God*, the British writer A. Alvarez described his own battle with depression. Having left his wife and child in England to accept a teaching job in America, Alvarez was extremely unhappy and slowly fell victim to a feeling of suffocation and despair. He wrote:

> My life felt so cluttered and obstructed that I could hardly breathe. I inhabited a closed, concentrated world, airless and without exits. I doubt if any of this was noticeable socially: I was simply more tense, more nervous than usual, and I drank more. But underneath I was going a bit mad. I had entered the closed world of suicide, and my life was being lived for me by forces I couldn't control.

Slow deaths

Alcohol and drug abuse are also common suicide triggers. Like depression, they are not direct causes of suicide, but they often play an important role. The suicide rate among alcoholics is much higher than the general population: Estimates indicate that between 7 and 21 percent of all alcoholics kill themselves, compared to less than 1 percent of the general population.

Studies show a link between alcohol abuse and the desire to end one's life. Indeed, the suicide rate among alcoholics is much higher than among nonalcoholics.

A person does not need to be a drug addict or alcoholic to be at high risk for suicide. Only about a third of all suicide victims had a history of severe alcohol or drug abuse. However, mind-altering chemicals can make a vulnerable person more prone to suicide. Since alcohol is a depressant, for instance, it can cause an already depressed person to feel even worse. It also lowers inhibitions, with the result that people are more impulsive and quicker to act on their emotions.

Autopsy reports very often show the presence of drugs or alcohol in the remains of suicide victims. Studies indicate that nearly half of all teenage suicides were under the influence of alcohol or drugs when they killed themselves. Kurt Cobain, who was struggling with heroin addiction at the time of his death, was a prominent example of a drug-related suicide.

Sometimes chemical abuse itself can be a form of suicide. In such cases, the drug or alcohol abuse becomes a kind of passive suicide, a slow death. By telling themselves that they are simply using drugs or alcohol to ease the pain of their lives, people can commit suicide without openly admitting it. Those who choose this route, in the words of writer A. Alvarez, "want to die without accepting the responsibility for their decision."

Slow death can come from diseases other than addiction. An estimated half million Americans, mostly young white women, suffer from anorexia nervosa—a mental disorder that causes them to stop eating and literally starve themselves to death. Although anorexia can often be treated, 15 percent of acute anorexics will die of the disease. Perhaps the most famous anorexic death was that of Karen Carpenter, who rose to fame in the 1970s as part of the musical group the Carpenters.

The underlying emotions of anorexia, such as alienation, hopelessness, and low self-esteem, are often strikingly similar to those of suicidal depression, alcoholism, and drug addiction. In his book *The Enigma of Suicide*, writer George Howe Colt quotes a young anorexic woman.

> "I didn't think I was worth anything," she said after dropping from 120 to 80 pounds. "I had no friends, no one to talk to. I was really depressed. I wanted to kill myself. I had thought of taking a knife or pills, but I couldn't. That was suicide, and I knew suicide was a sin. So I just stopped eating."

Family and peer influences

Many experts feel that a chaotic home environment can be a trigger for depression and suicidal behavior, especially in teens. If a family is loving and close-knit,

Hopelessness and low self-esteem are emotions that may foster self-destructive, suicidal behavior. These feelings are commonly associated with anorexia nervosa, an eating disorder that affects an estimated half million Americans.

chances are good a child can grow up with enough self-esteem to develop a healthy mental attitude, thus running a lower risk of suicide. But an abusive family situation, in which a child is constantly belittled or victimized, can lead to feelings of rage, violence, hopelessness, worthlessness, and despair later in life.

Suicidal behavior cannot be inherited from parents. However, just as people can inherit factors that put them at high risk for heart disease or diabetes, it is possible to inherit genetic tendencies for mental illnesses such as severe depression. A person with a family history of suicide is at a statistically higher risk for suicide. Studies indicate that people with such backgrounds are much more likely to commit suicide than the general population.

A poor relationship with family or peers can also trigger suicide by creating feelings of rage or revenge. Some people are so angry and vengeful toward family or friends that they feel compelled to punish them by committing suicide. "They'll be sorry when I'm gone" is an expression often heard by professionals who work with suicidal people. Other suicidal people may be motivated by despair; for example, an abused woman might see killing herself as the only way to escape an intolerable domestic situation.

Suicide attempts can be a way of trying to control the actions of others. One young man wanted to quit college and go to work, but his parents insisted that he finish his education. He felt he could get back at them by deliberately overdosing on sleeping pills. He knew he was not taking enough to kill himself, but he calculated (correctly, as it happened) that his parents would be so frightened when they found him unconscious that they would agree to his demands. His reasoning was that if they did not cave in, they would fear he would try again—and succeed.

Loss

Another major trigger for suicide is the loss of something important. Sometimes these losses are tangible and easily understood, such as the loss of one's health or the death of a close relative or friend. Sometimes a loss is not easily understood by an outsider. A crushing loss to one person may seem like a trivial matter to another. For example, people have killed themselves over failed tests and lost pets. Such losses, which most people can take in stride, were overwhelming to the persons who died.

A serious illness such as cancer or AIDS, or a physical disability such as multiple sclerosis, is a terrible psychological and physical experience. Many people who are in physical anguish choose to kill themselves, rather than suffer years of pain. The elderly, in particular, are at risk in this area.

The loss of a close family member or friend can also trigger suicide. Many elderly men and women become severely depressed when their spouses die. They may feel inadequate to the job of continuing life without their mate. Some therapists feel that the premature loss of a child is

A man mourns the death of a friend. The death of family and friends can be devastating, triggering suicidal behavior in people who are unable to cope with the loss.

the worst thing a parent can suffer, and parents who experience the death of a child may become suicidal.

Losing a job may also trigger suicide. Unemployment can lead to an emotional downward spiral driven by loss: the loss of self-worth, of status in the community, of a sense of financial and emotional security, even of family and friends. This tailspin, if not stopped, can lead to suicidal depression. Following the stock market crash of 1929, many businessmen killed themselves rather than face a jobless future in which they would lose expensive homes and fine possessions and be unable to support their families.

Even the loss of one's job upon retirement can be a trigger. For many older people, especially men who have devoted their lives to their jobs and have few outside interests, forced retirement is devastating. A person who has been wrapped up in a job for many years often becomes so strongly identified with work that its ending shatters feelings of individual identity.

Coercion and mass suicides

Every once in a while someone is forced to commit suicide. The coercion may result from psychological pressure imposed by a group such as a cult. Or it may be more subtle, as in cases of suicide pacts between lovers.

There have been only a few instances of mass or group suicides in the Western world. Most of them come about because of shared religious beliefs. One famous instance occurred in A.D. 73, when 960 Jews chose death over slavery to the Romans. During the Second World War, a group of young European women known as "the ninety-three maidens" took poison rather than fall prey to Nazi invaders. More recently, in 1978, followers of self-styled religious leader Jim Jones drank cyanide-laced Kool-Aid at Jonestown, their compound in Guyana in South America; 911 people died.

Studies of suicide pacts between lovers or family members indicate that they are often murder-suicides. The dominant partner, usually a man, convinces his partner to join him in death. The distinguished novelist Arthur

Koestler wrote, "There is only one prospect worse than being chained to an intolerable existence: the nightmare of a botched attempt to end it." Two years later, in 1985, Koestler killed himself at the age of seventy-seven. His wife, Cynthia Jeffries, apparently unable to bear the thought of life without him, joined him in a suicide pact.

No single explanation

Even when all these theories and common triggers are considered, there is no single explanation for suicide. Killing oneself can be triggered by any of several factors, or a combination of them. The roots of suicide, meanwhile, are so tangled that it is impossible to find one satisfactory explanation.

Many experts believe that there is no single cause of suicide. Nor, they feel, will any single means of research discover a satisfactory answer. Instead, they argue, the answer probably lies in an interconnected approach. In the words of psychiatrist Herman van Praag of the Albert Einstein College of Medicine, "Suicide is a three-dimensional problem involving psychology, sociology, and biology."

2

Teen Suicide

SUICIDE IN ANY form is a serious problem, but the issue of suicide among young adults is especially serious. Many experts feel that teen suicide has reached epidemic proportions.

In the last thirty years, the rate of reported suicides among teens in America has tripled. It now stands at about 16 per 100,000 for boys and 4.2 per 100,000 for girls. Suicide is the third leading cause of death (after accidents and homicides) among fifteen- to twenty-four-year-olds. From these figures, it appears that every year about five thousand young Americans kill themselves. The real number may be much higher, since families sometimes try to conceal a suicide, and many deaths that are officially classified as accidental may in fact be suicides.

A still larger number of young people—estimates range from half a million to 2 million yearly—try to kill themselves but do not succeed. Accurate records of attempted suicide are unobtainable, but studies indicate that for every adolescent suicide there may be twenty or more unsuccessful tries—perhaps 120,000 every year. This is about twice the estimated figure for adults.

Many studies have been done on teen suicide. It has been found that teens usually prefer to use firearms; one study indicated that some 60 percent of teen suicides are the result of gunshot wounds. One study estimated that 2 percent of all high schoolers have made at least one suicide attempt. Another found that half the teenagers questioned had "seriously considered" suicide by the time they graduated from high school. In another study, 58 percent said they knew someone who had attempted suicide, and 10 percent claimed to have made an attempt.

The issues around teen suicide are in some ways similar to suicide in general, but there are important distinctions. Perhaps the most crucial is a rise in the rate of teen suicide that not only is rapid but is much greater than that for the general population. Some experts identify this troubling trend as a symptom of a general failure in moral and religious codes and changing family structures.

Others blame it on violence in the media and on easier access to alcohol, drugs, and guns. Stress at school and the pressure to succeed in an increasingly competitive world are the bases of other theories. Some people, meanwhile, feel that the recent emphasis on suicide prevention acts as a suicide trigger, actually making things worse by encouraging immature people to discuss the delicate subject. On

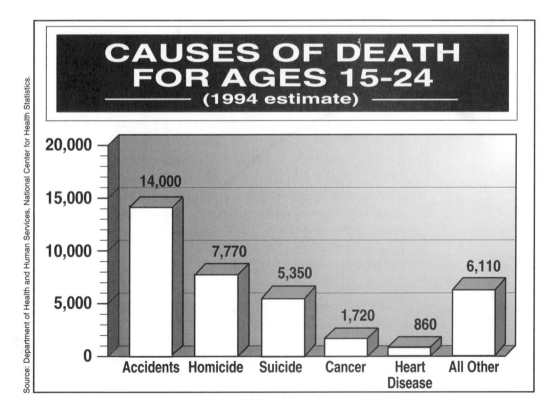

Source: Department of Health and Human Services, National Center for Health Statistics.

CAUSES OF DEATH FOR AGES 15-24
(1994 estimate)

Cause	Deaths
Accidents	14,000
Homicide	7,770
Suicide	5,350
Cancer	1,720
Heart Disease	860
All Other	6,110

the other hand, many experts think that too little discussion aggravates the problem.

None of these factors by itself is a cause for suicide, or for the rapid increase in the teen suicide rate. Perhaps the underlying cause is a combination of them all. Taken together, these conditions all add to the general stress level for teens, and so put vulnerable young people at greater risk.

A number of risk factors and triggers are considered to be especially crucial to teen suicides. Among these are depression, drug and alcohol abuse, sexual abuse or other problems within the family, problems stemming from sexual identity crises or other forms of isolation, and the suicide of someone close, which can be a trigger for so-called cluster or copycat suicides.

Depression

Young people are especially vulnerable to depression. One study concluded that in terms of frequency, depression was second only to the common cold among teens. According to the National Institute of Mental Health, depression is most likely to appear for the first time between the ages of fifteen and nineteen.

Many people who work with teenagers consider periodic, short-lived depression a normal part of growing up. Teens are at a stage in life characterized by finding one's individuality, personal identity, and place in the world. According to psychiatrist Paul Walters, director of health services at Stanford University, "I think that depression, in a funny way, is an inevitable part of adolescence. In fact, if you don't get depressed, I think there's something wrong."

Problems arise when adolescents fail to realize that depression will almost always go away. Depressed teens may keep the sadness bottled up, refusing to let anyone see what they fear is a sign of weakness or craziness. Teens in such a situation worry that they will never feel normal again. These feelings can create a high risk of suicide. According to psychologist Douglas Powell,

It's important to help [young people] realize that it's perfectly possible to have a date that isn't earth-shattering and that even if it's not such a great time, you're still the same person afterward and it's not the end of the world.

Only a very small percentage of depressed teenagers choose suicide. This leads some experts to believe that most youth suicides result from other forms of mental illness. Psychiatrist Barry Garfinkel has estimated that 90 percent of the teens who commit suicide were experiencing forms of mental illness more extreme than depression. "Kids don't commit suicide just because they've been harshly treated or life's dealt them a bad hand," Garfinkel has remarked.

The ways in which young people react to life's challenges, Garfinkel has argued, point to the deeper causes of suicidal behavior. One such response mode is a group of psychological problems commonly called conduct disorders. Young people with conduct disorders display symptoms such as impulsive behavior, substance abuse, problems with authority, and difficulty controlling anger. As writer Nancy Wartik has noted, "When such youths take their lives, researchers see it as 'violence turned inward.'" Some experts suspect that a low amount of serotonin in the brain may play a role in conduct disorders, although medical research on serotonin has so far largely been carried out on adults.

Drugs and alcohol

Drug and alcohol abuse is one of the most serious problems facing young people. The U.S. Department of Health and Human Services estimates that some 5 million adolescents—about one-third of the total number—have drinking problems. Experts consider chemical abuse to be a major trigger in teen suicide.

Studies have shown a clear link between chemical abuse and suicide in teens. Autopsy reports reveal that almost half the young people who commit suicide are under the influence of alcohol or other drugs shortly before death. The same is true for roughly one-third of those who attempt but do not complete suicide.

Young people are especially vulnerable to drug and alcohol abuse, which can add to the potential for suicide.

Chemical abuse by itself does not cause suicide in young people. Millions of teenagers drink and use drugs but do not kill themselves; for a few young people, however, drugs and alcohol can act as a trigger. Chemicals offer a chance to withdraw from reality and an opportunity to step toward suicide, perhaps heightening aggressive behavior and lowering inhibitions, so that teens become even more vulnerable to depression or self-destructive behavior.

One New York teenager, a good student from a close-knit family, became involved with a group that was heavily into drinking and drugs. Alienated from his family and under the influence of alcohol and other substances, he tried twice to kill himself but failed. Despite the youth's insistence that he did not have a problem, his parents made him enter a drug rehabilitation program, which helped him change his behavior and need for drugs and alcohol. In addition, a staff psychologist helped him talk about and understand the self-destructive feelings he had experienced since childhood. Now an adult, this former substance abuser is a counselor in a similar program, helping young people who are experiencing what he once went through.

Family and peer problems

Studies suggest that a child who grows up in a troubled household is more likely to have problems as a teen. Therapists often encounter family-oriented problems in suicidal teens, such as the loss of a parent through divorce, death, or desertion; fighting between family members; physical, sexual, or emotional abuse; poor communication; and frequent moves. A child who grows up in a family with a history of mental problems, or of alcohol and drug abuse, is also at a higher risk for suicidal feelings.

The autopsy report on one young man who had hanged himself showed no drugs and only a little liquor in the body at the time of death. There was, however, a family

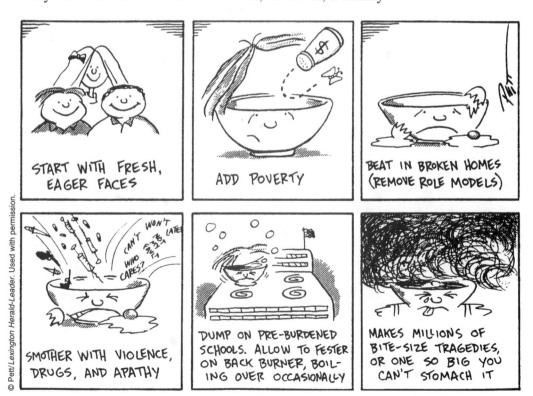

history of alcoholism, and one sister later remarked, "Eddie never wanted to be a part of us." Another sister added, "I felt partly to blame for his death, because he tried to get me to stop drinking so many times. I never listened to him. I was into drugs, too. It wasn't until four years after Eddie passed away that I got the message and went into rehab."

Many experts feel that divorce and broken homes are major factors in putting teens at risk for suicide. There is no direct evidence of this, but several studies indicate connections. The divorce rate in the United States has tripled in the last 30 years—the same growth rate as teen suicides. About half the marriages in America end in divorce, while about 70 percent of teenagers who attempt suicide come from broken families. According to psychologist Calvin Frederick, "The primary underlying cause of the rising suicide rate among American youth seems to be a breakdown in the nuclear family unit."

Negative attitudes and hostility toward gays particularly affect gay youth. Studies indicate that gay and lesbian teens are choosing to end their lives in alarming numbers.

Family problems are only one aspect of an overall stressful environment that can foster depression and even suicide in teens. Pressure to succeed at school and in athletics, where competition breeds stress, are other common situations for teens. For most people, these stresses never become so great that they create suicidal feelings. However, in some cases they can be tremendous. One young woman, the daughter of two physicians, desperately wanted to follow her parents in their profession. When she was not accepted into any medical school, she became so distraught that she could see no alternative but to take an overdose of sleeping pills.

Still another pressure young adults commonly face is simply that of being part of a large group who are competing for a limited number of jobs, college openings, and other positions. The teenage population in this country is especially large just now, and some experts pinpoint the stress caused by this competitive atmosphere as another cause of the increase in teen suicide.

Gay and lesbian teens

Gay and lesbian teens are at especially high risk for suicide. Studies indicate that these groups are two to three times more likely to attempt suicide than other teens. According to a report by a presidential task force, suicide is the leading cause of death among homosexual teens. It has been estimated that one-third of all gay and lesbian teens attempt suicide, and over half experience suicidal feelings at some point in adolescence.

In general, gay and lesbian teen suicide is caused by a set of problems very different from those leading to overall teen suicide. Research by the Los Angeles Suicide Prevention Center indicates that suicide attempts and completed suicides among gay teens are usually prompted by long-standing sexual anxieties and fears, rather than by an event (such as the death of a parent or the breakup of a relationship) that is not necessarily related to their sexuality.

Most teens have a difficult time with all the usual problems of growing up. Family life, social groups, school, an uncertain job future, and many other conditions can combine to make life confusing. For gay and lesbian teens, the burdens are even greater. They must struggle to find and accept their sexual identity in an atmosphere that is often hostile. They often feel compelled to keep their true nature secret from even their closest friends. If they have had a strict, deeply religious, or conservative upbringing, they may experience crushing self-doubt and self-hatred.

As a result, gay and lesbian teens often feel especially isolated, lonely, scared, trapped, and outcast. They often lack sympathetic social support systems available to other teens, such as drop-in centers. They can be harassed, ridiculed, and even assaulted at school. One college student felt the only way he could handle his attraction to other men was to hide it beneath his role as a star basketball player. He thought his friends and family would never understand. "I let them think I was nothing more than a jock," he recalled. "I couldn't let anyone see anything more." He tried to fit in by socializing with girls but was confused about what to do on dates. He had only one sexual encounter with a man, which left him terrified that he had contracted AIDS.

Increasingly depressed and distraught over his conflicting feelings, he finally wrote a note to his family and tried to kill himself by inhaling car exhaust in his garage. His sister discovered him before the carbon monoxide had proved fatal, however, and called paramedics. Months of hospital rehabilitation left the young man confined to a wheelchair and further limited by permanent brain damage. However, after a period of intense anger and grief, he has finally begun to talk about his feelings, even his previously hidden sexual urges. He later remarked, "I know that to get healthy in my head, I need to talk about what I'm feeling. That's a big part of what makes living worthwhile."

TV and movie violence

Many people feel that violence in the media and elsewhere can act as a suicide trigger for some young people.

Recently there has been considerable attention paid to explicitly violent song lyrics, movies, computer games, books, and television shows. There is no evidence that this violence directly causes suicide, but critics of media violence argue that it makes death seem commonplace, casual, romantic, or even funny.

Opponents of this view argue that censoring ultraviolent song lyrics, movies, TV shows, or computer games will do nothing to cut down on suicide. They argue that inflammatory music, movies, and literature do not cause violence; they are simply reflections of what is happening in the world. Furthermore, they say, even the most violent or inflammatory expressions should be protected under the First Amendment, which protects the right to free speech.

The burden of society's antigay sentiment may be more than some gay teens can endure. These friends and family members hold a memorial service for an eighteen-year-old gay student who chose to end her life.

Several movies have been singled out as possibly having spurred suicides. *The Deer Hunter*, an Oscar-winning film about Vietnam veterans that contains a scene of Russian roulette, was linked by researchers to nearly fifty Russian roulette deaths. Two other popular films, *An Officer and a Gentleman*, in which a young naval cadet hangs himself, and *Dead Poets Society*, in which a prep school student commits suicide because he cannot withstand pressure from family and peers, are among those that have been linked to real suicides.

Another area of controversy is music. One musician who is often singled out is rocker Ozzy Osbourne, whose lyrics seem to promote suicide. In "Suicide Solution," Osbourne sings, "Suicide is the only way out / Don't you know what it's really all about." This song has figured in at least one death: In 1984 a nineteen-year-old Californian shot himself with his father's pistol while listening to

Friends of two students who killed themselves as part of a suicide pact console themselves during a memorial service. Teenagers seem especially susceptible to group, or cluster, suicides.

"Suicide Solution" repeatedly on headphones. The boy's father sued Osbourne and the record company, claiming that the "violent, morbid, and inflammatory music . . . encouraged [him] to take his own life." The suit was later dismissed.

Controversy over suicide triggers in popular entertainment is nothing new. Every generation has outrageous and controversial figures like Ozzy Osbourne. Two hundred years ago, the German writer Johann Wolfgang von Goethe was accused of inspiring a suicide epidemic. Goethe's novel *The Sorrows of Young Werther*, published in 1774, is about a depressed young man who shoots himself over his impossible love for a married woman. The book was an immediate sensation, and young men all over Europe imitated Werther's flamboyant way of dressing and his sensitive style of speech. Like Werther, some of them also shot themselves because they thought it was a beautiful, romantic final gesture—an adventure of sorts.

Cluster suicides

For unknown reasons, teen suicides sometimes occur in groups. The death of one teen in a group seems to spur others to kill themselves soon afterward. These deaths are commonly called cluster suicides.

Cluster suicides do not occur only among teens. There have been many other instances, especially in confined settings with rigid social structures such as prisons, colleges, army barracks, and mental hospitals. But teens seem to be particularly at risk.

One of the most prominent examples of a teen suicide cluster began in 1983, when eight teenagers in Plano, Texas, a wealthy suburb of Dallas, killed themselves, one after the other. The triggering event was the death of one boy in a car crash. The first teen apparently was a victim of the form of suicide sometimes called "auto-suicide," in which people deliberately execute fatal crashes. Seven more students in the same town committed suicide within fourteen months. No particular social group seemed to be singled out; among those who died were the high school football captain, a cheerleader, and several delinquents and loners.

No one can explain why cluster suicides happen. One theory is that adolescents tend to be highly suggestible and are especially prone to imitating others. Another theory links clusters with the tendency to report sensational news and violence on television. Critics of television news argue that reporting on suicide tends to give it an aura of celebrity or glamour.

There is no direct evidence to prove it, but critics charge that repeated media coverage of a suicide may be a factor in cluster suicides. Troubled teens may see highly publicized or sensationalized coverage of a death and realize that the act of killing themselves will succeed in drawing the attention of family, friends—and the evening news. One high school counselor has commented:

> I don't suggest that the media stop reporting suicide, but they have a responsibility not to romanticize it. The line between reporting and romanticizing suicide is easy to draw—[it depends on] whether it's splashed on the front page with a romantic headline or put on page four with the basic facts.

On the other hand, some experts say, the right kind of publicity and open discussion about suicide may benefit teenagers, by making them more aware of the need to seek help if they are at risk. Memorial assemblies at school and sensitively written movies are examples of this sort of public acknowledgment. Another example is the series of public service announcements that have appeared on television in recent years, in which sports figures, famous musicians, and movie stars urge teenagers to choose life.

Cries for help

Suicide attempts are often a means of indirectly crying out for help. Teenagers are especially prone to using suicide in this way. One psychiatrist has used the phrase "a desperate version of holding their breath until turning blue." In other words, it is a kind of emotional blackmail—do what I say, pay attention to me, or I'll kill myself. The reasons for taking such a drastic step vary. Perhaps other, more rational ways of asking for help have failed, or perhaps the teen simply doesn't know how to ask in a normal way. It may appear that the only way to draw attention is a suicide attempt.

Like some adults, teenagers sometimes plan their attempts to ensure that they will be discovered in time. One thirteen-year-old Illinois girl slashed her wrists in the bathtub a week after her father moved out of the house, timing the act to coincide with her mother's expected arrival in the bathroom. The girl later told a therapist that she had hoped her action would help bring her parents back together. "I didn't really want to die," the girl said later. "I just hoped and prayed that if Mom and Dad knew how upset and unhappy I was, Dad would move back in."

As is true for our society as a whole, female teenagers are much more likely than males to make incomplete suicide attempts. Also like

society as a whole, successful suicide victims are mostly male. A sixteen-year-old Minnesota boy felt that his father devoted more time and attention to his Cadillac than to his kid. One night the teen left a note saying that he was an outcast at school. He stole the keys to the Cadillac and drove it into a tree.

After several months in the hospital recuperating from his injuries, the boy came home but found that little had changed. Eight months after his first attempt, he succeeded in killing himself by means of carbon monoxide, inhaled behind the wheel of his father's Cadillac.

Instant cures

Teens tend to be more impulsive than adults, and a suicide is often triggered by, for example, a bad report card, a broken prom date, a fight with parents over curfews—seemingly trivial events involving conditions adults don't have to worry about. Such an event is usually not the real reason a teen commits suicide, but it can be a trigger—the final straw that drives him or her over the edge.

To an adolescent in pain, suicide can seem like an instant cure. In one short moment, all the pain will go away. However, this is irrational; it is "like treating a cold with a nuclear bomb," as one therapist put it. According to the director of a suicide prevention agency in Massachusetts,

> When young people are suicidal, they're not necessarily thinking about death being preferable, they're thinking about life being intolerable. They're not thinking of where they're going, they're thinking of what they're escaping from.

Like some adults, teenagers often indulge in what therapists call "magical thinking." Suicidal adolescents may not understand that death is permanent. They may think of it as a sanctuary, a kind of sleep, or a vacation. They might agree with Peter Pan that "to die will be an awfully big adventure."

Magical thinking makes people believe in irrational or impossible things. For instance, a fifteen-year-old girl came into a Lawrence, Massachusetts, suicide prevention center recently. In one pocket she carried a bottle of sleeping pills, and in the other a bottle of ipecac, a liquid that doctors use to make infants vomit. She told a crisis worker, "I want to kill myself, but I don't want to be dead. I mean, I want to be dead, but I don't want to be dead forever, I only want to be dead until my eighteenth birthday."

One of the real tragedies of teen suicides is that the problems that can lead a teenager to suicidal thoughts, especially the sort of immature or incomplete thinking called magical thinking, usually could have been resolved with time and therapy. And yet of the thousands of suicidal teenagers in America, only a fraction—perhaps 10 or 20 percent—will seek counseling or other professional help. And of all the teens who try to kill themselves and fail, 10 percent will try again and succeed.

3

Is Suicide Ever
an Acceptable
Solution?

MANY PEOPLE FEEL that suicide can never be justified, that it is never an acceptable way to solve a problem.
To people who hold this view, no one ever has the right to
take a life—even his or her own. Suicide, for them, is simply wrong. On the other hand, many people argue that
choosing the time and manner of one's death is like choosing the way one lives—a basic human right that should always be respected. In between these views are many
shades of opinion and feeling.

If there is any agreement in the debate, it is probably on
the question of when suicide is *not* acceptable. Most
experts and others would argue that suicide is a poor
solution for temporary problems and even for many long-
running difficulties. In these cases, there is nearly always
a less drastic solution than suicide. For example, a fight
with a girlfriend or boyfriend can be extremely upsetting,
and so can the loss of a job. But such problems are temporary. As a rule, these crises can be resolved over time,
usually with the aid of counselors, doctors, members of
the clergy, family, and friends.

It is important for even severely depressed people to understand that most crises and periods of depression will
pass and that life will eventually improve. As psychiatrist

George Murphy put it, "The desire for life . . . will return even in a patient who cannot believe that such a change can occur."

Any discussion of suicide as a solution to life's problems is likely to become entangled in a variety of deeply held beliefs about life, and to touch on thorny problems of philosophy, religion, medicine, and the law. People have been thinking and talking about this issue for centuries, and there is still no single answer.

A tragically premature choice

Probably the most widespread argument against suicide as a solution to problems is that it goes against deeply rooted religious beliefs of many people.

The ancient Jews introduced to western society the belief that God created everything, including life; therefore, everything—including everyone's body and spirit—belonged to God, and suicide was a serious sin. This view of the sanctity of human life later became a cornerstone of Christianity. In the fifth century, Augustine summed up this Judeo-Christian attitude when he wrote that the commandment "Thou shalt not kill" was specifically meant to prohibit killing oneself, as well as others. Opposition to suicide on religious grounds is very common today.

Another argument against suicide as a problem solver is that there is always hope for people in despair. For example, a depressed person suffering from a deadly disease may regain the strength to go on living by focusing on the possibility that a cure will be discovered in time. Too often, many experts say, suicide is a tragically premature choice.

There are many examples of people who considered suicide, decided against it, and went on to great achievements. As a young man, Abraham Lincoln was severely depressed after (temporarily) breaking off his engagement to Mary Todd. He contemplated suicide, but decided to live. When physician George R. Minot was diagnosed with severe diabetes, for which there was then no successful treatment, he thought about killing himself.

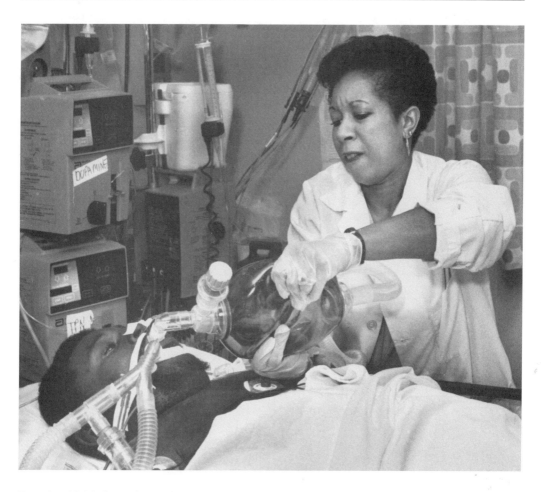

But in 1923 insulin was discovered, Minot was saved, and eleven years later he won the Nobel Prize in medicine for his research on anemia.

And sometimes miracles do occur. Cures for life-threatening diseases have been found. Cancer patients go into remission. People suffering from terrible diseases discover that with proper pain management they can continue to live in relative comfort. The chance of such seemingly miraculous events occurring is a strong argument against suicide even where illness is concerned.

Whether suicide may be justified is a topic that is hotly debated. Some argue that people who are in physical anguish should be able to kill themselves, rather than suffer years of pain.

Death with dignity

However, a growing number of people in this country view suicide as an acceptable solution to at least one problem: terminal illness. According to this view, any conscious and consenting adult should have the right to end his or her life if faced with a painful or severely debilitating terminal illness. This philosophy is often called "death with dignity."

Suicide under these circumstances has a long history of advocates. One of them was the Roman statesman and philosopher Seneca (4 B.C.–A.D. 65), who said, "If I can choose between a death of torture and one that is simple and easy, why should I not select the latter? As I choose the ship in which I sail and the house which I inhabit, so I will choose the death by which I leave life." Like many Roman and Greek philosophers, Seneca was generally opposed to suicide but felt that in the case of severe illness it was justified and even constituted a noble way to die.

Today, sophisticated medical technology can extend the lives of some seriously ill patients for years and virtually free them from pain. However, death-with-dignity advo-

IT WOULD BE CRUEL TO PROLONG tHE INEVITABLE.

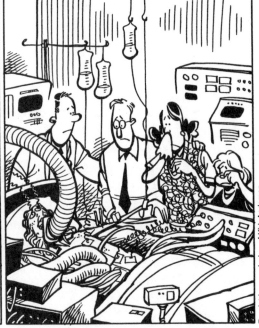

IT'S INEVITABLE TO PROLONG tHE CRUELTY.

cates say that the quality of life for a terminally ill person can be so poor that death is often preferable. They argue that people should be allowed to choose the time, setting, and circumstances of their deaths.

The person could then prepare friends and family, make final arrangements, and depart in a sedate, painless, predetermined manner. Pierre Ludington, the executive director of the American Association of Physicians for Human Rights, began stockpiling pills and planning his death when he discovered he was HIV-positive. He has said,

> I get angry that society wants me to suffer in a hospital. . . . I envision having a wonderful meal with friends. After they leave, I'll sit in front of the fire listening to Mozart, mix everything with brandy, sip it, and somebody will find me.

One prominent group advocating the right to die is the Hemlock Society, founded in California in 1980 by a British-born journalist, Derek Humphry, who had helped

Author Derek Humphry advocated the right to die—and generated considerable controversy—with the publication of his book Final Exit, *a how-to suicide manual.*

his terminally ill first wife take her own life. Humphry's explicit manual for suicide, *Final Exit*, became a best-seller in 1991 and was the focus of considerable controversy. Humphry is no longer associated with the society, but he remains firm in his belief that suicide is a legitimate choice and "an intimate, personal, libertarian decision."

Should physicians assist death?

The debate over suicide in the case of terminal illness becomes even thornier when physicians are added to the equation. One of the most basic premises of medicine

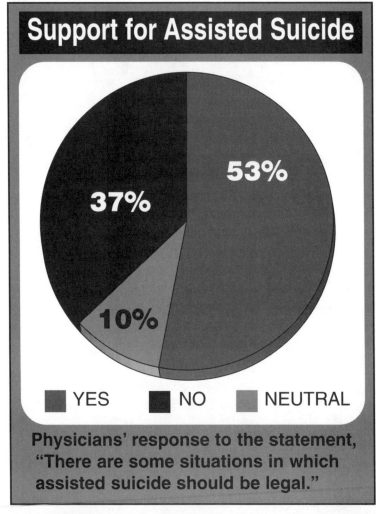

Support for Assisted Suicide

53%

37%

10%

■ YES   ■ NO   ■ NEUTRAL

Physicians' response to the statement, "There are some situations in which assisted suicide should be legal."

Source: *The New England Journal of Medicine*, July 14, 1994.

states that doctors must do anything and everything to ensure the well-being of their patients. The Hippocratic oath, the twenty-five-hundred-year-old creed of physicians, states in part, "I will give no deadly medicine to anyone if asked, nor suggest any such counsel."

But many people, some doctors and nurses included, have challenged this notion. "If a doctor's obligation is to relieve suffering," they ask, "are there cases when helping a patient die quickly is better than keeping that person alive but helpless, hooked up to life-support systems and perhaps in pain?" State and federal government agencies, hospitals, and individual physicians are deeply divided on the question. Meanwhile, polls indicate that a growing number of Americans think doctor-assisted suicide should be legalized; that is, doctors should be allowed to hasten the death of those who wish for it but cannot accomplish the act alone.

It is not legal in this country for a physician or anyone else to assist in a suicide, but an increasing number of doctors have been quietly doing so, by such means as allowing their patients to stockpile pills. These doctors are following the example of physicians in the Netherlands, who for years have been allowed to help their patients commit suicide under supervised circumstances. Meanwhile, a recent *Boston Globe* poll showed that 64 percent of the public favors letting doctors give lethal injections to the terminally ill.

However, many doctors are outraged by this idea. They argue that doctor-assisted suicide will always be wrong. "Medicine is a profession dedicated to healing," the American Medical Association has declared in an official statement. "Its tools should not be used to kill people."

Doctors who oppose so-called assisted suicide argue that recent developments in medicine mean that no one has to suffer pain. Pain control has advanced so much, they say, that anyone who is in pain is a victim of improper medical care. With correct amounts of medication and humane social services such as hospice care, a terminally ill person can almost always die in relative peace and comfort. As Dr.

In a news conference, Dr. Jack Kevorkian (right) describes assisted suicide in detail. Kevorkian views suicide as a basic human right and continues to advocate what he terms "death with dignity."

Joanne Lynn, a noted specialist in aging and dying, put it, "It is an outrage for us to seriously discuss killing the sufferer rather than relieving the suffering."

"Doctor Death"

One of the most prominent figures in the controversy over physician-assisted suicide is Dr. Jack Kevorkian. Kevorkian is a retired Michigan pathologist who in 1990 connected an Alzheimer's patient to a "suicide machine" he had devised. When the patient pushed a button, the device pumped poison into her bloodstream. Kevorkian has since assisted in about thirty suicides. Many, though not all, of those people had been diagnosed as having some type of terminal illness.

Kevorkian, who has become famous as "Doctor Death," uses the media attention from the suicides he has facilitated to voice his passionate beliefs about death with dignity. Although Kevorkian feels he is simply upholding the physician's promise to relieve suffering, many of his peers think he is playing God, deciding who should live and who should die. As George Annas, a professor at Boston University's School of Medicine, comments from another angle: "Death is still seen [by physicians] as the enemy. And that's what Kevorkian throws in their face. What he says is, 'Some people want death, and I am going to give it to them.'"

Legislating suicide

Arguing about death with dignity from a religious, ethical, or medical viewpoint is difficult enough. The legal aspects of the question make it even more complex.

Federal and state regulations are a bewildering and often contradictory tangle. One important federal law requires that patients admitted to hospitals be asked whether they want to sign a living will—a document that allows people to specify, in advance, that they do not wish to be treated with certain procedures, called heroic measures, that would prolong life artificially.

However, this law is interpreted quite differently from state to state. In some states, only competent, mentally alert people can make a decision about heroic measures. In others, doctors and relatives are allowed to "pull the plug" in the case of patients—for example, those in deep and irreversible comas—who cannot personally request it.

Two recent decisions by the U.S. Court of Appeals will affect how legislation is made in the future. In 1996 the court for the Ninth Circuit, which is responsible for nine western states, struck down a Washington State law that made assisted suicide a felony. Soon after, the Second Circuit Court of Appeals struck down a similar law that affected three northeastern states. The decisions were major victories for the right-to-die movement. If nothing else, they will probably force the medical profession and others to continue debating this emotional issue.

Meanwhile, the movement to legalize doctor-assisted suicide is gathering popular support. In several states, including Washington and California, public initiatives to legalize assisted suicide have failed very narrowly. Similar laws will be up for vote again in these and other states.

The right-to-die controversy

The debate over the right to die is, in some ways, similar to the abortion question. Both issues address some of society's most basic and passionately held feelings about life and death, right and wrong. Both probe the role of families and doctors in making decisions for patients, and both question assumptions about the rights of individuals. Judge Stephen Reinhardt, in writing the majority opinion for the Ninth Circuit Court ruling, even quoted the Supreme Court decision on abortion when he wrote,

"[T]he decision how and when to die is 'one of the most intimate and personal choices a person may make in a lifetime,' a choice 'central to personal dignity and autonomy' [independence]."

Like the abortion question, death with dignity may become one of the most important and controversial debates of our time. As *Newsweek* writer Katrine Ames put it, "Most of us have some choice in how we live, certainly in how we conduct our lives. How we die is an equally personal choice—and, in the exhilarating and terrifying new world of medical technology, perhaps almost as important."

4

After a Suicide

SUICIDE HAS BEEN called a "victimless" act—that is, one that punishes only the person who commits it. But in fact many people are deeply affected whenever someone commits suicide. It has been estimated that in America every year the lives of a quarter million people besides the victims are directly affected by suicide. These people, often called suicide survivors, are the ones left behind.

People who experience the death of someone close normally go through a period of intense grief and mourning after the initial shock wears off. In time, most people move on with their lives. One woman whose father shot himself because he was terminally ill grieved for about a year before her life was back to normal. For others, such as the brothers and sisters of a college-age woman who killed herself by slashing her wrists, the period of mourning can last much longer. "It feels," the victim's brother said, "as though my pain—our pain—will never go away. It's been three years now. Maybe someday we'll all be back to normal, but somehow I think it will always be with us."

Grief

Grief gives mourners a period of distancing, allowing them to separate themselves emotionally from the person who has died. As Freud put it, "Mourning has a quite specific psychical [psychological] task to perform: its function is to detach the survivors' memories and hopes from the dead."

There is no customary or normal length of time for the grieving process. Some people never fully recover and spend the rest of their lives in mourning. Others can go back to their usual lives, functioning more or less as before, within a few months or even weeks. A study by the National Academy of Sciences found that most people grieve for one to three years after losing a family member through suicide or other cause of death.

Suicide survivors are left to cope with a wide array of emotions, including sadness, guilt, and even anger.

Two of the most common emotions experienced by people grieving after a suicide are shock and depression. Immediately following a suicide survivors usually go into shock, which temporarily deadens normal emotions and produces a sense of unreality, numbness, and unresponsiveness to the attempts of others to help. In some ways, this is similar to the "disaster syndrome" experienced by survivors of earthquakes, plane crashes, and other catastrophes.

When the shock wears off, depression and sorrow are likely to set in. This period usually passes in a few months, although it is estimated that 20 to 30 percent of suicide survivors are severely depressed for a year or more after the death. Even so, it is a temporary phenomenon that usually can be treated with therapy and, if needed, antidepressant drugs. Physical symptoms, such as stomach pains, are also common reactions. "It was like a fist reached into my stomach and closed tight," one girl commented about the physical sensation following her best friend's suicide.

In the wake of a suicide, people often experience a wide range of other emotions. These include guilt, anger, shame, relief, confusion, and even suicidal feelings. These emotions do not have clear boundaries. People who are grieving often experience some or all of these emotions at the same time and find it impossible to separate them.

Guilt and anger

Guilt, a common reaction among survivors after any death, may be especially intense after a suicide. Survivors often feel directly or indirectly responsible for the act of self-destruction. The parents of a teen who shot himself may blame themselves for the rest of their lives, asking over and over how they could have failed their child. A young person whose mother or father committed suicide may grow up feeling that he or she somehow was responsible, hence guilty.

Guilt can be especially overwhelming if suicide has been committed for revenge. One man shot himself at home, leaving a note for his wife, with whom he had been quarreling, that blamed her for his death. In effect, he was saying, "Look what you made me do." The effect was devastating, as he had hoped it would be; less than a year later, the widow killed herself.

Even if they realize that no one was directly responsible for the suicide but the victim, people often still feel guilty simply because they are still alive. They obsessively examine their relationships with the dead person, hoping to find clues to the reasons behind the suicide or ways in which they could have stopped it. The thought that the death could have been prevented if only the right thing had been done in time creates even greater guilt. "I keep thinking, 'There must have been something I should have done differently,'" said one woman whose brother killed himself. "I should have seen what was coming, I should have been more alert. For the rest of my life, I'll probably wonder if things might have been different."

Also, survivors may feel guilty that they did not notice the warning signs of an impending suicide. They feel they should have been watching out for such signals every minute. This is an irrational thought pattern, because people do not normally take full responsibility for the lives of others who are able-bodied, mentally competent, and past early childhood. But people do not always think clearly when experiencing strong emotions. As a result, in the aftermath of a suicide people are often overwhelmed with guilt even if they understand that they are not to blame.

Anger is another common reaction during the grieving process. The people who are grieving may be furious with the dead person, for rejecting life with them and for deserting them. They may be angry at God for allowing the suicide to happen. They may be angry at themselves, other friends and family members, or the mental health profession for not doing more to prevent the final act. And they might be furious that life goes on—that the world does not come to a screeching halt because of their grief. When his girlfriend killed herself, one man remembered, he felt overwhelmingly angry.

I was furious! I was mad that she did this to herself, I was pissed off at myself that I could have let it happen, I was angry that her parents and her doctors couldn't help her. I was just so damned mad at everybody—and there was nothing I could do.

Shame and denial

Many people tend to think of suicide as a cowardly act, or as an embarrassment. Cruel jokes and angry words are sometimes spoken about suicides and their families. As a result of this social contempt, shame is a common reaction among survivors. To accommodate grieving families, or because police investigations are not complete, newspapers often omit the mention of suicide as the cause of death. Even so, families may withdraw from society, avoiding contact with neighbors and friends, because they are deeply embarrassed.

Denial is another common emotion. The desire to deny that a beloved friend or family member who was not terminally ill could have been so desperate as to commit suicide can be intense. Other people who are close to the grieving family are often willing to go along with this denial. Thus one couple, the night after finding the body of their son, who had hanged himself, went to the house of close friends for a dinner that had been arranged weeks before. The grieving parents kept the engagement because they felt it would be comforting to be with people who knew them well. As it turned out, however, the couples talked about the weather, sports, politics—anything but death. The hosts were afraid to mention the tragedy; the survivors didn't want to burden their friends. Most grief therapists agree that this form of blocked communication is not a healthy way to mourn a loss. It is better, they say, to allow the venting of emotions than to bottle these stresses inside.

The feelings of shame associated with suicide may come from inside the survivor, but they feed on the reactions of others. Writer George Howe Colt, in *The Enigma of Suicide*, quoted a woman whose teenage son had committed suicide. The mother felt the sting of the reactions of others even years later:

> Losing my son was painful enough, but the whispers, feeling like a leper, being avoided, having people not look me in the eye or acting like nothing happened, never mentioning the death, changing the subject, people being afraid it's contagious, as if it may happen to them if they touch me or reach out to me—is almost worse.

Some people grieving a suicide are so ashamed and afraid that they even wonder whether funeral services should be held. They may fear the victim is not worthy of such attention. Most therapists, however, feel that giving up a memorial service will only delay the healing process. They argue that the lives of loved ones should be celebrated without regard to the manner of death, because even the most painful or sad life contains some happiness and love.

Memorial services can help friends as well as family deal with a suicide of someone close. A service can also show friends of the family that their support is needed and welcome. Friends may be afraid to talk about the suicide to the family, or to lend other support. But such offers may be an important part of healing for everyone. Support may be as simple as a compassionate conversation, but it can also take the form of practical help such as running errands or cooking meals. Writer Adina Wrobleski, who herself is a survivor of the suicide of a close family member, has this advice for the friends of someone who is grieving:

> Don't be afraid of suicide survivors; the worst that can happen is someone might burst into tears. Put your arm around him or her, and give comfort. Don't give into the embarrassment and shame society imposes on suicides and their families. Reject the notion that suicide results from "bad" and "sick" families. In most cases of suicide, someone in the family was very sick and died. The rest of the family is well.

Relief

It may seem strange that a common feeling among people in the wake of a suicide is a feeling of intense relief.

Friends remember an eighteen-year-old student who made the tragic decision to end her life. The effects of a suicide can be devastating to family and friends.

But this is a common reaction if the victim had a long history of aggressive behavior or deep unhappiness.

Some people who committed suicide were violent alcoholics, abusive parents or spouses, serious drug abusers, or mentally ill patients who spent their lives in institutions. For the family and friends of such people, suicide may signal the end of a long, exhausting, miserable battle. One schizophrenic man killed himself after four attempts, many hospitalizations, and years of instability in the face of an abundance of therapy or family support. Afterward, his brother admitted to feeling better now that it was over. "We all felt some relief," he said. "He had been so unhappy, and now he was out of his pain. I felt my brother had finally taken some sort of initiative and been successful at something."

Many survivors are surprised to experience feelings of relief, which can create even more guilt: "How could I be glad she's dead? I must be an awful person." Grief counselors tell the family and friends of suicide victims that a feeling of relief does not signify lack of love or concern for the victim. Instead, they say, it is usually a healthy sign of awareness that years of tense, fearful uncertainty are over.

Suicidal thoughts in survivors

Many survivors must at some point come to terms with suicidal thoughts of their own. Research indicates that the risk of suicide among people grieving a suicide is eight times higher than in the general population. There is no known single reason for this higher rate; it is probably the result of a combination of factors.

There is no hard evidence that suicide can be inherited. However, there is strong evidence that people can pass on to their children a genetic susceptibility to certain mental illnesses, such as schizophrenia and depression, that can trigger suicide.

Also, many suicidologists feel that suicide is a learned reaction in some families. Once suicide has occurred in a family, they argue, that one act may serve as an example. Just as abused children tend to become abusive parents, a parent's suicide may give a child the idea that killing oneself is an acceptable way to deal with a deeply distressing situation. In 1961, suffering from depression and alcoholism, the writer Ernest Hemingway shot himself—thirty-three years after his father had shot himself and eleven years before his younger brother, who had found their father's body, also killed himself.

Family members during the grief process are at a higher risk for suicide for other reasons as well. They may be plunged into a severe depression. Fearing this gloom will never go away, they can become suicidal. Other factors may also play a part, such as a desire to join the dead person or extreme feelings of guilt. In such extreme cases,

While every individual grieves a suicide in a different way, feelings of intense grief and sadness are common.

another suicide may appear to be the only way to end the pain. As psychologist Robert Jay Lifton put it in his book *The Broken Connection*, "Despair and hopelessness are associated with perceptions of the future. . . . Whatever future one can imagine is no better, perhaps much worse, than the present."

The devastating effects of suicide on young people

Every person who mourns a suicide feels the loss in an individual way. It is devastating to each one. But the effect of suicide on children may be the most severe of all.

Study after study has shown that the loss of a parent in early childhood, especially by suicide, can have a dramatic impact on a person's psychological development. Children are amazingly resilient, but of course they lack mature coping skills. A suicide by a parent often triggers short-term problems in childhood and adolescence, such as delinquency, learning disabilities, and self-destructive behavior, as well as severe problems later in life, including depression and psychosis. According to a National Academy of Sciences report on grief, "For children, the suicide of a parent or sibling not only presents immediate difficulties, but is thought by many observers to result in life-long vulnerability to mental health problems."

Feelings of guilt

Children are especially susceptible to guilt. They may think that they are responsible for a death because of something they said or did, or even because they thought bad thoughts. As one child therapist remarked, "Kids are apt to take the blame for any death. They feel they might have been responsible for it because of something they thought or wished or said or did or didn't do."

Too often adults leave children alone with their grief, or keep the truth about the cause of death from them. These adults are usually well-meaning, wanting only to shield the children from pain. But lack of communication can leave a child's imagination to fill in the blanks, and fearful imaginings can be worse than the truth: "I killed Daddy because I was thinking bad thoughts about him." "Mommy died because she didn't love me anymore."

Research also suggests that it is unhealthy to disguise the true cause of death from children. One boy who found his father hanging was told for years by family members that there had been a fatal car accident. The boy grew up extremely confused, torn between the memory of what he had seen and what the grown-ups told him.

Working through grief

Not all survivors need therapy. It is possible for individuals and families to work through grief on their own. Often, however, therapy is crucial if people are to remain

Students participate in a class dealing with adolescent stress in Plano, Texas, a city that has been plagued by teen suicide. The teachers hope not only to end this tragic trend, but also to help the teens cope with their grief.

healthy in the aftermath of a suicide. A counselor or therapist can do a great deal to help work through suicidal thoughts, depression, and other feelings.

Individual therapists deal with problems of grief in different ways. However, the current trend in therapy emphasizes open, honest, sensitive discussion of the death. Therapists generally feel that if guilt and anger remain bottled inside, the chances of another suicide or other inappropriate reactions are much greater.

Psychological problems associated with grief can be so strong that mourners may be afraid they are going crazy. It is not uncommon for them to think they see the dead person walking around, to hear his voice or his key in the door, even though they know rationally that such things are impossible. Here therapy can also help the survivors work through their emotions.

Many forms of long-term therapy are available if needed. Some people grieving after a suicide find that anti-depressant drugs help them cope. Support groups, made up of people in similar situations, are also at hand. In many cases, however, the old saying "Time heals all wounds" is more or less true. As a rule, the period of mourning passes, and people are able to resume routine lives with the help of friends and family.

Some therapists feel, however, that survivors never fully recover. Thoughts of the dead person may seem to disappear temporarily, but the memory will always remain with the survivor in some form. Sometimes memories, which may be painful or pleasant, will surface in unexpected ways. The triggering event may be as important as a birthday or as trivial as a favorite TV show. Because of these memories, many people who have suffered loss through suicide feel as though their daily lives will never be the same. As one man whose wife hanged herself put it, "Life is back to normal, but normal is different now. Normal will never be the normal it was before a year ago."

Keeping the spirit alive

Usually the impulse to keep a suicide victim's spirit alive is a balanced and normal part of grieving. But it can sometimes become an unhealthy obsession, with remaining family and friends unable to talk of anything else or to maintain normal lives. Some families, for instance, preserve the dead person's room exactly as it was, leaving the bed unmade or the schoolbooks on the desk.

The opposite reaction is to maintain denial too long. Some people avoid mentioning the dead person and get rid of all of his or her possessions. When survivors shut themselves off from reality in this way, communication with the outside world—especially with other friends and family—may close down completely. One man refused to mention the name of his father, who had killed himself. He could not bring himself to talk about the suicide with his wife and children, even though he had been a teenager at the time of the tragedy. It was as though the father had never existed.

Most therapists would agree that these two extremes are not healthy ways to deal with a painful subject. Dwelling too much on questions that can never be answered keeps people from carrying on with their lives. Stony silence is just as unhealthy.

Generally, a middle ground can be found. After the suicide of a teenage boy, most of the surviving family retreated into awkward silence. For months no one talked about the youth at all, although his mother joined a support group. Several months went by, and serious problems began to surface. The surviving children were getting into trouble with the law and at school, and the parents barely spoke to each other.

When the mother realized that her family was falling apart under the strain of avoiding the subject, she persuaded them to seek help together. In therapy the family discovered that each one had wanted to talk about the death for a long time. Everyone but the mother, however, had rejected the idea of getting help out of fear of upsetting the others. In therapy, parents and siblings talked openly about the anger, sorrow, and guilt they all felt. The family was able then to begin rebuilding the mutual love and trust that had broken down during the months of silence.

Life goes on

A period of mourning is a major disruption in life. Eventually, however, small but significant signs of change start to appear, indicating a shift back toward normal life for survivors. The changes may start as soon as a few weeks after the suicide, or they may be much longer in coming. A typical sign of recovery might be a mother's change from visiting her daughter's grave daily to going to the cemetery once a week.

The gradual easing of the pain is normal and healthy, although some people say that the relief itself makes them feel guilty again. They worry because they are not thinking about the victim twenty-four hours a day. One woman whose sister committed suicide remarked, "I keep

In the wake of a suicide, survivors are sometimes left with a sadness that they fear is impenetrable.

thinking that if I can go on with my own life, then I must be a terrible person. Maybe I should be punished, because why should I be happy when she's dead? I know it's not rational to think that, but I do."

Each survivor reacts individually. Though most resume their lives, others are changed forever by the suicide of someone close. The death becomes the most significant moment in their lives, the event that defines everything else. One such person was a college-age woman whose fiancé, a gifted painter, killed himself. For the rest of her life, the woman wore black and kept a shrine to her dead lover in her room. Her life was ruled by his death.

Studies indicate that long-term grief can have serious effects on physical as well as mental health. Smoking, drinking, and drug use often increase dramatically. Men who have lost someone close are at an extremely high risk for death from accidents, heart disease, and infectious illnesses. Women are at less risk overall, perhaps because they are more likely to seek professional help and to rely on support networks during difficult times. Still, the risk for women of such diseases as cirrhosis of the liver (a deadly illness caused by excessive drinking) tends to rise following the death of someone close.

Positive changes

Despite the devastating effect of suicide on those remaining, in a strange way the experience can sometimes be positive. Some survivors have discovered beneficial changes in their family relationships; a shared tragedy can draw a family closer together, making them more loving, attentive, and compassionate. Others, as they fight to regain their lives and work through their grief, find inner strength they had not known existed. They realize that if they can survive the self-inflicted death of someone close, they can make it through anything.

A woman whose husband shot himself remarked, "Maybe we're never quite the same people we were before. But maybe that's not all bad. Maybe we wouldn't want to be that person." After grieving the death, this woman began to do things she never did before: leading a survivors' group, returning to graduate school, fulfilling her dream of becoming a writer. She feels that she is now a better, kinder, more thoughtful, and more positive person. Though she is grateful for these changes, she is also aware of the price she paid: "I'd give them up in a minute if I could have him back."

How a survivor chooses to live after a suicide depends on many factors, some of which may be beyond the person's control. In any given situation some matters must be left to others. Often, however, the most important of these factors can be controlled. As writer Adina Wrobleski put it,

> While one cannot bring the person back, and while there are no second chances with the person who died, there are many second chances with the living. There is an opportunity to make up in the present what is desperately wished for in the past. The death of a loved one changes people; how they change is up to each individual.

5

Preventing Suicide

MOST PEOPLE WHO are seriously thinking about suicide show certain typical warning signs. Sometimes, people who are suicidal try to hide their true feelings from themselves and others, covering up and doing their best to act normal. It may seem to survivors, therefore, that suicide happens unexpectedly.

Experts say, however, that in almost every case of suicide there were clues that the survivors overlooked (or saw but did not acknowledge). Therapists who deal with suicide feel that many needless deaths can be avoided by learning better how to recognize and deal with these warning signs. The ability to recognize these signs and act on them could mean the difference between life and death.

Suicidologists and other experts have developed many methods of spotting suicidal behavior and minimizing the chances of completing a suicide. These diverse methods include research studies, education on suicide prevention, safety precautions such as guardrails on high bridges, and emergency centers—suicide hot lines, for example. Although a truly determined person can almost never be stopped from committing suicide, a combination of some or all of these preventive measures will work in many cases.

Basic warning signs

Suicide is seldom an impulsive decision. Most of the time it is premeditated; that is, the person thinks for a long time about whether and how to commit suicide before actually doing it. When in a suicidal frame of mind, people usually display one or more typical behavioral patterns. Basic clues that a person is considering suicide can vary from a clear verbal sign ("I'm so miserable I'm going to kill myself") to a sudden change in behavior, such as unexpectedly giving away possessions.

Suicide is difficult to predict even for a skilled psychiatrist or suicidologist, and these warning signs and clues are not ironclad. Not everyone who exhibits typical warning signs is necessarily suicidal, and not everyone who commits suicide shows obvious warning signs. However, in the vast majority of potential suicide cases, some warning signs are present. If in doubt, experts say, it is always better to err on the safe side: to assume that a troubled person is indeed considering suicide.

The single best indicator of possible suicide is a previous attempt. People who have already tried to take their own lives make up the highest risk group for following through successfully. In fact, the suicide rate for repeat attempters is more than six hundred times higher than for the general public.

COMMON WARNING SIGNS

A suicidal person may:

- ▶ Talk about committing suicide
- ▶ Have trouble eating or sleeping
- ▶ Experience drastic changes in behavior
- ▶ Give away prized possessions
- ▶ Have attempted suicide before
- ▶ Take unnecessary risks
- ▶ Have had a recent severe loss

- ▶ Be preoccupied with death and dying
- ▶ Lose interest in personal appearance
- ▶ Increase use of alcohol or drugs
- ▶ Lose interest in hobbies, work, school, etc.
- ▶ Withdraw from friends and/or social activities
- ▶ Prepare for death by making out a will and final arrangements

Source: American Association of Suicidology

Suicidal talk is another basic indicator. People who commit suicide usually talk about it first. Typical statements include, "They won't have to worry about me any longer" and "I'm going to jump off that bridge if you leave me." Suicidal people often reveal carefully thought-out plans about how they will kill themselves. Experts say that any talk about suicide, even something said jokingly, should be taken seriously. The idea that people who talk about committing suicide never actually do it is a myth.

Careful final arrangements comprise another basic warning sign. Suicidal people often put their affairs in order before they take their lives. This might mean making a will, giving away important possessions, writing elaborate notes, or arranging for the care of pets. People who are putting their affairs in order before committing suicide often act and speak as if they are preparing for a long journey.

A sudden, major change in a person's personality or behavior can also be a clue. Unusual nervousness, angry outbursts at inappropriate times, lack of interest in appearance and health, or an unexpected decline in school performance or attendance can be signs of deeper problems. Another sign is a sudden shift in interests—perhaps a dedicated jogger suddenly gives up running. An abrupt change in personality is one more possible symptom—for example, a friendly, outgoing person may become withdrawn and moody for a long period.

Depression and suicide are closely linked. The risk of a depressed person committing suicide is some fifty times higher than for a person who is not depressed. Clues indicating severe depression can therefore also be warnings of potential suicide. Among the typical signs of depression are extreme sadness, excessive crying, sleeplessness, loss of appetite, withdrawal from everyday life, and a feeling of hopelessness or emptiness.

Depressive changes can also be physical: a sudden change in weight or sleep habits, extreme fatigue, and inability to concentrate, make decisions, or remember things. In the case of teenagers or children, behaviors such as frequent truancy or disobedience may also be signs. Long-term sadness, low self-esteem, and aggressive behavior are also common signals of depression in teens. Depression in teens is difficult to spot, however, since mood shifts are a part of every young person's normal development.

The appearance of one of the common symptoms of depression is not necessarily a cause for concern. Many experts feel, however, that two or more warning signs together are a clear signal of possible danger. If the warning signs are noticed during a time of major stress, there is even greater reason for concern. One normally cheerful Seattle-area teen was having a rough time at home because her parents were in the process of a messy and bitter divorce. She went through strange mood shifts, slept long

Depression is the most commonly identified suicide trigger. Talking to a friend or counselor may help alleviate depression and suicidal thoughts.

hours, and lost her passion for skiing, causing her friends to worry about her.

Although the teenager shrugged off her changing moods and apathetic attitude, her friends recognized the possible signs of depression and persuaded her to see a counselor. The counselor helped this young client recognize that there were serious issues at home that she needed to deal with, and together they were able to work them out.

What to do

Therapists stress that listening is the single most important thing anyone can do to help a suicidal person. People who see that someone is depressed, or hear that person talk about suicide, should not make light of the circumstance or ignore it. They should not assume that troubled people talk about suicide just to get attention.

Suicidal people above all need empathy and to be taken seriously, say the therapists. Depression is a disease, they continue, and a depressed person needs understanding and support just like any other ill person. In his book *Darkness Visible*, which deals with his own battle with suicidal depression, novelist William Styron wrote:

> The pain of severe depression is quite unimaginable to those who have not suffered it, and it kills in many instances because its anguish can no longer be borne. The prevention of many suicides will continue to be hindered until there is a general awareness of the nature of this pain. Through the healing process of time—and through medical intervention or hospitalization in many cases—most people survive depression, which may be its only blessing; but to the tragic legion who are compelled to destroy themselves there should be no more reproof [blame] attached than to the victims of terminal cancer.

It is a mistake, experts feel, to tell a depressed person something like "Lighten up." Saying that someone's feelings are foolish or unworthy, hoping he or she will snap out of a prolonged period of sadness, will often make things worse. And telling suicidal people that they have good lives or "everything to live for" may only increase their depression and guilt. Suicidal people are in such emotional pain that it is impossible for them to appreciate the positive parts of their lives. As writer George Howe Colt put it, telling a suicidal person to just cheer up "is like telling someone with two broken legs to get up and walk."

Depressed people need a friend's sympathetic ear, but they also need frank, nonjudgmental discussion. Friends who are dealing with a suicidal person should repeat back what the person says, making sure it is understood clearly. They should ask direct questions. Many therapists suggest using fairly blunt questions such as, "Are you thinking about harming yourself?" If the answer is yes, the friend should ask whether the suicidal person has a plan. If so, the friend should try gently to find out what it is.

If the friend feels that the danger is immediate, and especially if there are weapons available, the suicidal person should not be left alone. If possible, weapons should be removed from the scene. Many people plan to do away with themselves by a certain method. If that method is not available, they may not resort to others. For instance, if a man who plans to shoot himself cannot get access to his gun, he might well postpone his suicide—thereby opening a window for help through crisis intervention or other means.

Crisis intervention

The next step is to get professional help. The friend should suggest that the suicidal person call a suicide prevention center, or offer to accompany him or her to such a facility. Depending on the situation, a talk with a sympathetic teacher, clergyman, doctor, or other trusted authority may be appropriate. If the suicidal person refuses, the friend should get help. If not near a telephone, the friend may have to invent a story or otherwise induce the person to go to a place from which help can be summoned.

Experts say that people dealing with potential suicides should not be afraid of seeming disloyal, even if the suicidal person is a close friend and tries to hold others to secrecy by saying "If you're really my friend, you'll promise not to tell." When people are feeling hopeless, their judgment is impaired. What may seem like disloyalty, breaking a confidence, or going behind someone's back could turn out to be a courageous act of lifesaving.

Most depression, and most suicidal thoughts, will go away over time and with proper help. This knowledge forms the basis for suicide intervention, the process of preventing a suicide from occurring. If a person can be calmed and kept safe, the suicidal state of mind will almost certainly pass. In extreme cases it may be necessary to use force, with the suicidal person kept in a locked room or otherwise restrained.

Some depressed people seek professional help to get them through hard times and teach them to manage negative feelings.

Organizations devoted to suicide intervention are called crisis centers. The first crisis centers opened in the late 1950s, and today about two hundred centers in the United States provide places where people who are suicidal, distraught, or isolated can find someone to talk to via telephone hot lines and drop-in facilities. The crisis center may be staffed by psychiatrists or other professionals; quite often, however, volunteers are trained in helping people talk about their problems. The largest organization of this type, the Samaritans, started in England and now has offices in over forty countries.

Usually a crisis-line counselor works directly with a client, but sometimes the help is indirect. Recently a fifteen-year-old girl called a San Francisco line in tears. Her boyfriend was suicidal because he was going to fail school. He had told the girl he had a shotgun and was going to kill himself, but made her promise not to tell anyone.

The therapist first calmed the girl, convincing her that she had done the right thing by breaking this promise. The girl felt that contacting the boy's parents would not help, since the mother had virtually given up on him and the father was an abusive alcoholic. She also felt that her own parents could not help, because they disliked her friend.

The therapist asked the girl to make sure someone trustworthy would stay with the suicidal person all day. The therapist then telephoned the school counselor, who called the boy into his office. Without mentioning anything about suicide or crisis lines, the counselor said he had been looking at the student's grades and offered to enroll him in summer school, which would improve his grades without hurting his permanent record. The boy was surprised to discover that there was a way out of his problem. He passed through the immediate crisis without harming himself and successfully completed summer school.

Most crisis facilities are not equipped to provide long-term care. People who need more than emergency help are referred to clinics or other facilities for treatment. Often, however, solving the immediate problem is enough—and sometimes all that is needed is a sympathetic ear. As one crisis worker put it, "All you can do is listen, really listen. That's what people need when they're hurting."

Long-term help

Once the immediate crisis has passed, a suicidal person may need long-term help. Most therapists say that a suicide attempt is a symptom, not a diagnosis, of larger problems. In other words, the suicidal feelings were indicative of profound personal difficulties. The goal of long-term help is to treat these underlying problems.

Although some suicidal people have no clearly definable underlying illness, usually the problem is some form of depression, which can be treated by means of psychotherapy, drugs, and, if necessary, hospitalization.

There are many different types of psychotherapy. Sometimes the client is seen alone by a therapist or psychiatrist. Sometimes family members are included. The suicidal person may also participate in group counseling sessions. Group therapy can be especially valuable in reducing feelings of isolation. "The person realizes she's not alone—everyone else in the room has had suicidal thoughts," says one psychologist who works with such groups. "The issue of suicide loses its impact. We talk openly about suicide, but we can focus on other, healthier options."

The use of antidepressant drugs can dramatically relieve severe depression. However, these agents also have serious and powerful side effects. Since the drugs are usually prescribed together with some form of psychotherapy, the patient can usually be monitored by a physician to make sure the side effects do not become extreme.

Most experts feel that hospitalization in a mental institute is a last resort for suicidal people. Psychiatric hospitals have a suicide rate over five times greater than that of the general population, according to Norman Farberow, a pioneer suicidologist. He points out that the extreme confinement in these hospitals and battles over control between patients and staff drive many hospitalized patients to take their own lives.

Experts agree that long-term care is the most important single component in treating self-destructive behavior. They also agree, however, that there is no single cure—that even the most carefully designed, individualized treatment is no guarantee that a suicidal patient will never be suicidal again. As Farberow puts it,

> Drugs [and other forms of treatment] are an essential part of medical management of suicidal patients. However, drugs alone cannot be counted on to prevent suicide. The most important elements are human relations, psychologic[al] support and constructive action.

Education

Crisis intervention and long-term therapy can be very effective for individual cases of suicidal behavior. The problem of reducing the suicide rate in general is a much more broad and complex topic.

Educating the general public about suicide is one important element of this issue.

Many organizations, such as the American Association of Suicidology, the American Suicide Foundation, and the Family Service Association of America, regularly sponsor seminars, programs in public schools, and other forms of educational outreach. Recently, there has been a strong focus on teaching teens about suicide prevention through films, slide shows, public service announcements, and classes. Nearly half of all U.S. teens now participate in suicide prevention classes.

These educational programs can be extremely graphic. The goal is often to shock teens into awareness by showing the ugly reality of suicide. One program developed by Victor Victoroff, chief of psychiatry at Huron Road Hospital in Cleveland, Ohio, features grisly color slides of teens who have made suicide attempts—a girl's bloody wrists, a boy's face destroyed by a shotgun blast—and emergency medical equipment, such as tracheotomy kits used in hospitals, which contain the tools for cutting breathing holes in throats to try to save people who have attempted to kill themselves.

Victoroff's program has two main points: to show that suicide is far from romantic, and to demonstrate that hospitalization for a suicide attempt is a most terrifying experience. He also talks about the horrors of botched attempts, which include permanent physical impairment such as blindness, brain damage, or paralysis. "I want them to know," Victoroff has said, "that playing around with suicide is a dangerous game [and] that suicide is not romantic at all. It's hard and dirty—and it involves a lot of heartache and agony."

Some experts fear that suicide prevention classes may backfire and make the subject seem more appealing.

These critics worry that talking about suicide openly might increase the number of suicides, stirring up dangerous feelings in vulnerable students and thus bringing about precisely what the classes are designed to prevent. However, the overwhelming trend in suicide prevention classes is to talk about the issue openly and frankly.

Improvements in society

Individual intervention, crisis lines, therapy, and suicide prevention classes can all be very effective. But some experts say that even more far-reaching and fundamental changes in society will be necessary to stop suicide.

A number of proposals have been put forward in this regard. Some suicidologists have called for improved education in elementary schools to help children learn such basic life skills as setting realistic goals, improving self-esteem, and using humor to get through difficult situations. Improved education for parents should be another long-term goal, they add, since a parent who understands and listens to kids' concerns will help prevent self-destructive behavior. And many people feel that the situation will improve with increased funding for medical and psychological research into self-destructive behavior.

Some suicidologists also feel that physical changes will help. Emergency telephones and barriers on high bridges, nets on observation decks, and nonopening windows in high buildings are examples of what is sometimes called "environmental risk reduction." Psychologist Richard Seiden has compared changing the environment as well as the individual to saving lives by reducing traffic accidents: "There is more than one approach to suicide prevention. . . . It's the same as automobile safety. You can do driver training and you can [also] make the car safer." Some critics, however, say that such changes will only delay a person bent on suicide.

Programs such as stricter gun control and a more sensitive approach to prescribing potentially lethal drugs have also been proposed. And some experts have called for even more basic changes in society. They worry about

No one knows for sure what makes some people want to die. Many people agree, however, that increased education can help children learn skills to help them get through difficult situations.

increased isolation, fearing that the suicide rate will rise as a result of declines in close family structures and the influence of organized religion, and in rises in factors such as computer network use, joblessness, and neglect of the elderly. A more closely integrated, satisfying, and fulfilling society may be the answer to suicide. As George Howe Colt put it, "[O]ne might reduce the suicide rate by giving people more reasons to stay alive."

The slender thread

In the 1965 movie *The Slender Thread*, Sidney Poitier plays a crisis-line volunteer who helps a woman, played by Anne Bancroft, through a suicidal episode. The title refers to the thin line of human compassion that connects people, even complete strangers, to each other. Too often, this line is the only thing that stands between a desperate person and death.

Education, research, and social legislation may do a great deal to reduce the suicide rate. However, the single most important element in suicide prevention is still the human connection. Fortunately, this connection—the desire to help others live—can usually be found in our society. George Howe Colt suggests that a few twisted people in a crowd may shout "Jump!" to a suicidal person on a building ledge. Many more, however, will cry out, "Live!"

Organizations
to Contact

American Association of Suicidology
4201 Connecticut Ave. NW, Ste 310
Washington, DC 20008
(202) 237-2280

This is a professional association of people such as therapists and psychologists who are concerned with suicide research and prevention. It also operates as a national clearinghouse for information on suicide by publishing and distributing material on suicide.

American Medical Association (AMA)
535 N. Dearborn St.
Chicago, IL 60610
(312) 645-5076

The primary professional association for medical doctors. The AMA has a special committee that studies suicide from a medical perspective. It also provides information on medicine and public health care.

American Psychiatric Association
1400 K St. NW
Washington, DC 20005
(202) 797-4900

A professional organization for the psychiatric field. It has an extensive range of materials on suicide available to the public.

American Psychological Association
1200 17th St. NW
Washington, DC 20036
(202) 833-7600

A professional organization for psychologists. Like the other professional organizations, it is a source of information and educational materials on psychological research.

American Suicide Foundation
1045 Park Ave.
New York, NY 10028
(212) 410-1111

An organization that supports suicide prevention through research and education. It has a range of material on suicide available to the public.

Family Service Association of America
44 E. 23rd St.
New York, NY 10010
(212) 674-6100

Among other services, this group provides information on counseling for suicide survivors.

The Hemlock Society
PO Box 66218
Los Angeles, CA 90066
(213) 391-1871

A nonprofit educational organization that supports the right-to-die movement and provides information on legal and legislative developments to the public on the topic.

National Committee on Youth Suicide Prevention
825 Washington St.
Norwood, MA 02062
(617) 769-5686

This group acts as a central point for a network of professionals, officials, and individuals who are concerned with reducing the incidence of teen and adolescent suicide. Provides a range of materials and information on the issue.

National Institute of Mental Health
5600 Fishers Lane
Rockville, MD 20857
(301) 443-3877

A branch of the federal Public Health Service. Provides information and resources on suicide research and prevention programs.

The Samaritans
500 Commonwealth Ave., Kenmore Square
Boston, MA 02215
(617) 247-0220

The American branch of the largest nonprofessional organization committed to helping suicidal people. The Samaritans maintain walk-in clinics and hot lines in communities around the world. The Boston headquarters is also a source of information on suicide and suicide prevention.

Society for the Right to Die
250 W. 57th St.
New York, NY 10107
(212) 246-6973

An advocacy group for passive euthanasia and the right of the terminally ill to death with dignity. A source of information on such issues as living wills and legal aspects of the right-to-die movement.

Youth Suicide National Center
445 Virginia Ave.
San Mateo, CA 94402
(415) 655-1974

This group coordinates and supports activities aimed at suicide prevention among young people. It develops and distributes educational materials and other resources on this topic.

Suggestions for Further Reading

Michael Biskup, ed., *Suicide: Opposing Viewpoints*. San Diego: Greenhaven Press, 1992. A series of readings and articles for young adults on the subject of suicide.

Laura Dolce, *Suicide*. New York: Chelsea House, 1992. A general book on suicide, for young adults.

Judith Galas, *Teen Suicide*. San Diego: Lucent Books, 1994. A book concentrating on teenage suicide, for young adults.

Sandra Gardner, *Teenage Suicide*. New York: Julian Messner/Simon & Schuster, 1985. A book concentrating on teenage suicide, for young adults.

Margaret O. Hyde and Elizabeth Held Forsyth, M.D., *Suicide*. New York: Franklin Watts, 1991. A general discussion, for young adults.

Susan Kuklin, *After a Suicide: Young People Speak Up*. New York: G. P. Putnam's, 1994. Interviews with a variety of young suicide survivors and people who have attempted suicide.

John Langone, *Dead End: A Book About Suicide*. Boston: Little, Brown, 1989. A general overview, for young adults.

Jane Mersky Leder, *Dead Serious*. New York: Macmillan, 1987. An excellent book about teenage suicide, written for teenagers.

Judie Smith, *Coping with Suicide*. New York: Rosen Publishing, 1986. For young adults.

Adina Wrobleski, *Suicide: Why? 85 Questions and Answers About Suicide*. Minneapolis, MN: Afterwords, 1995. Not specifically for young adults, but contains clear and concise explanations of many common questions. Written by a suicide survivor.

Works Consulted

Lewis B. Aiken, *Dying, Death, and Bereavement*. Boston: Allyn & Bacon, 1985. A scholarly book by a university professor of psychology.

A. Alvarez, *The Savage God: A Study in Suicide*. New York: Bantam Books, 1973. A classic study of suicide by a British author who nearly committed suicide himself.

Katrine Ames, "Last Rights," *Newsweek*, August 26, 1991.

George Howe Colt, *The Enigma of Suicide*. New York: Summit/Simon & Schuster, 1991. A comprehensive look at all aspects of suicide by a distinguished journalist whose excellent writing illuminates this serious topic.

Anthony DeCurtis, "Kurt Cobain 1967–1994," *Rolling Stone*, June 2, 1994.

Norman K. Denzin, "The Suicide Machine," *Society*, August 1992.

Anne Fadiman, "Death News," *Harper's*, April 1994.

Stephen A. Flanders, *Suicide*. New York: Facts On File, 1991. A bare-bones but valuable compilation of facts and figures.

David W. Garrow, "The Justices' Life-or-Death Choice," *The New York Times*, April 7, 1996.

Nancy Gibbs, "Love and Let Die," *Time*, March 19, 1990.

———, "Rx for Death," *Time*, May 31, 1993.

Derek Humphry and Ann Wickett, *The Right to Die: Understanding Euthanasia*. New York: Harper & Row, 1986. One of several books written by a leader in the right-to-die movement and his wife (who later committed suicide).

Jack Kevorkian, M.D., *Prescription: Medicide*. Buffalo, NY: Prometheus Books, 1991. By the inventor of the "suicide machine," a leading voice in the right-to-die movement.

Tamar Lewin, "Ruling Sharpens Debate on 'Right to Die,'" *The New York Times*, March 8, 1996.

Robert Jay Lifton, *The Broken Connection*. New York: Simon & Schuster, 1980. A dense but fascinating book by the noted psychologist, who is an expert on suicide.

William McCord, "Death with Dignity," *The Humanist*, January/February 1993.

John Miller, ed., *On Suicide*. San Francisco: Chronicle Books, 1992. A collection of pieces about suicide by a variety of well-known writers, including Jorge Luis Borges, William Styron, Graham Greene, and Philip Lopate.

Brian O'Reilly, "Why Grade-A Execs Get an 'F' as Parents," *Fortune*, January 1990.

Cynthia R. Pfeffer, *The Suicidal Child*. New York: Guilford Press, 1986. A book by a psychiatrist that focuses on suicide in young children.

James Rachels, *The End of Life: Euthanasia and Morality*. New York: Oxford University Press, 1986. By a professor of philosophy at the University of Alabama.

Elisabeth Rosenthal, "Dead Complicated," *Discover*, October 1992.

Ritch C. Savin-Williams, "Verbal and Physical Abuse as Stressors in the Lives of Lesbian, Gay Male, and Bisexual Youth," *Journal of Consulting and Clinical Psychology*, February 1994.

Joseph P. Shapiro, "Death on Trial," *U.S. News & World Report*, April 25, 1994.

William Styron, *Darkness Visible*. New York: Random House, 1990. A moving, first-person account of a struggle with suicidal depression, by the author of *Sophie's Choice* and other novels.

Thomas Szasz, *The Second Sin*. Garden City, NY: Anchor/Doubleday, 1973. A discussion of suicide and the right to die by a psychiatrist who argues in favor of the rights of the mentally ill.

Nancy Wartik, "Jerry's Choice: Why Are Our Children Killing Themselves?" *American Health*, October 1991.

Robert N. Wennberg, *Terminal Choices: Euthanasia, Suicide, and the Right to Die*. Grand Rapids, MI: Wm. B. Eerdmans, 1989. By a professor of philosophy at Westmont College, Santa Barbara, CA.

Index

Adler, Alfred, 16
African Americans
  suicide rate of, 11
AIDS, 34
  as cause of suicide, 16–17, 23
alcohol, and suicide, 29–31
alcoholism, 16, 18–19
Alvarez, A., 19, 20
American Association of
  Physicians for Human Rights,
  45
American Association of
  Suicidology, 78
American Medical Association,
  47
American Suicide Foundation,
  78
Ames, Katrine, 51
Annas, George, 49
antidepressant drugs, 17–18, 76
Augustine, Saint, 42
auto-suicide, 37

Bancroft, Anne, 80
biological theories of suicide,
  17–18
The Broken Connection
  (Lifton), 60

Carpenter, Karen, 21
Carpenters (musical duo), 21
categories of suicide
  (Menninger), 16–17
chronic suicide, 16
clinical depression. See
  depression
cluster suicides, 38–40

media and, 37–38
Cobain, Kurt, 15–16, 20
Colt, George Howe, 13, 21, 56,
  73, 80, 81
crisis intervention, 73–76
  hot lines, 75
  organizations, 75–76

Darkness Visible (Styron), 72
Dead Poets Society (film), 35
death with dignity, 43–46
DeCurtis, Anthony, 16
The Deer Hunter (film), 35
depression
  antidepressant drugs, 76
  as cause of suicide, 18–19
  severe, 18–19
Doctor Death. See Kevorkian,
  Jack
drug abuse
  as slow suicide, 20
  as suicide cause for teens,
  29–31
Durkheim, Émile, 14

The Enigma of Suicide (Colt),
  21, 56
environmental risk reduction, 79
family influences can trigger
  suicide, 21–22
  for teens, 31–33
Family Service Association of
  America, 78
Farberow, Norman, 76–77
Final Exit (Humphry), 45, 46
focal suicide, 17
Frederick, Calvin, 32

Freud, Sigmund, 16–17, 52–53

Garfinkel, Barry, 29
gay and lesbian teens, and
  suicide, 33–34
Goethe, Johann Wolfgang von,
  36
grief, 52–53
guilt, 54–55
  children particularly
    vulnerable to, 60–61

Hemingway, Ernest, 59
Hemlock Society, 45–46
Hippocratic oath, 47
hospitalization
  as suicide prevention, 76
hot lines, crisis, 75
Humphry, Derek, 45–46

Jeffries, Cynthia, 25
Jones, Jim, 24
Jonestown mass suicide, 24

Kevorkian, Jack, 48, 49
Koestler, Arthur, 24–25

legislating suicide, 49–50
lesbian teens, and suicide,
  33–34
Lifton, Robert Jay, 60
Lincoln, Abraham, 42
listening, as therapy, 72–73
Los Angeles Suicide Prevention
  Center, 33
loss, as suicide cause, 22–24
Ludington, Pierre, 45
Lynn, Joanne, 48

major depression. *See*
  depression
mass suicides, 24
media
  cluster suicides and, 37–38
Menninger, Karl, 13, 16, 18

Minot, George R., 42–43
Murphy, George, 42

National Academy of Sciences,
  53, 61
National Center for Health
  Statistics, 11
National Institute of Mental
  Health (NIMH), 19, 28
Native Americans
  suicide rate of, 11
"ninety-three maidens" mass
  suicide, 24
Nirvana (band), 15

An Officer and a Gentleman
  (film), 35
organic suicide, 16–17
Osbourne, Ozzy, 35–36

passive suicide, 20
physician-assisted suicide,
  46–49
Poitier, Sidney, 80
Powell, Douglas, 28–29
Praag, Herman van, 25

Reinhardt, Stephen, 50
right-to-die controversy, 50–51

The Samaritans (crisis
  facilities), 75, 77
The Savage God (Alvarez), 19
Seiden, Richard, 79
Seneca (philosopher), 44
The Slender Thread (film), 80
slow-death suicides
  alcoholism, 18–19
  anorexia nervosa, 21
  drug abuse, 20
The Sorrows of Young Werther
  (Goethe), 36
statistics, 8–12
Styron, William, 72
suicide

aftermath of, 52–67
  anger, 55–56
  grief, 52–53
  guilt, 54–55
  relief, 57–58
  shame and denial, 56–57
  survivors and, 59–60
  working through, 61–67
  young survivors and, 60–61
attempts, 22
  by teens, numbers not
    known, 26
causes of, 14–16
  AIDS, 16–17, 23
  alcohol, 16, 18–19
    for teenagers, 29–31
  biological, 17–18
  coercion, 24–25
  depression, 18–19
  drug abuse
    for teenagers, 29–31
  media violence, 34–36
  peer influences, 21–22
    for teenagers, 31–33
  psychological, 16–17
education about, 78–79
is acceptable, 41–51
  con, 42–43
legislating, 49–50
pacts, 24–25
physician-assisted, 46–49
prevention, 68-81
  basic warning signs and,
    68–72
  crisis intervention and, 73–76
  education and, 78–79
  listening as therapy, 72–73
  long-term help, 76–77
  social change, 79–80
triggers for, 18–25
  cluster suicides, 38–40
  coercion and mass suicides,
    24–25
  depression, 18–19
  family and peer influences,

    21–22
  for teens, 28–36
loss, 22–24
  slow-death, 19–21
see also teen suicide

teen suicide, 26–40
  as cry for help, 38–39
  as instant cure, 39–40
  attempts, 26
  drugs/alcohol and, 20, 29–31
  is second leading cause of
    death, 26
  method of, 26
  number of in U.S., 26
  rate higher than others, 27
  triggers for
    cluster suicides, 38–40
    depression, 28–29
    drugs and alcohol, 29–31
    entertainment violence,
      34–36
    family and peer problems,
      31–33
    homosexuality, 33–34
therapy
  as long-term help, 76
  for survivors, 61–63
  suicide prevention, 72–73
triggers for suicide. *See* suicide,
  causes of

unipolar depression. *See*
  depression
U.S. Department of Health and
  Human Services, 29

Victoroff, Victor, 78

Walters, Paul, 28
warning signs of suicide, 68–72
Wartik, Nancy, 29
World Health Organization, 9
Wrobleski, Adina, 57, 67

About the Author

Adam Woog is the author of over a dozen books for young people and adults. He lives in Seattle, Washington, with his wife, a mental health therapist, and their young daughter.

Picture Credits

Cover photo: ©Uniphoto, Inc.
AP/Wide World Photos, 45, 62, 77
Archive Photos, 17
Corbis-Bettmann, 14
© Earl Dotter/Impact Visuals, 23, 43
© Rick Gerharter/Impact Visuals, 32
© David M. Grossman/Photo Researchers, Inc., 60
© Bettye Lane/Photo Researchers, Inc., 74
© Andrew Lichtenstern/Impact Visuals, 20, 30
© Ursula Markus/Photo Researchers, Inc., 80
© Brian Plonka/Impact Visuals, 21
Reuters/Corbis-Bettmann, 15
Reuters/John Hillery/Archive Photos, 48
© Susan Rosenberg/Photo Researchers, Inc., 65
© Lonny Shavelson/Impact Visuals, 18, 35, 58
© Steven Skloot/Photo Researchers, Inc., 71
© Kuni Takahashi/Boston Herald/Impact Visuals, 53
UPI/Bettmann, 39
UPI/Corbis-Bettmann, 9, 36